Creative Thought FORMS

Creative Thought FORMS

The Art & Science of Spiritual Transformation

MARK L. PROPHET
ELIZABETH CLARE PROPHET

SUMMIT UNIVERSITY PRESS®
Gardiner, Montana

CREATIVE THOUGHT FORMS
The Art and Science of Spiritual Transformation
Mark L. Prophet and Elizabeth Clare Prophet

For information: The Summit Lighthouse,
63 Summit Way, Gardiner, MT 59030 USA
1-800-245-5445 / 406-848-9500
TSLinfo@TSL.org
www.SummitLighthouse.org

Library of Congress Control Number: 2022934592
ISBN: 978-1-60988-398-0
ISBN: 978-1-60988-399-7 (eBook)

SUMMIT UNIVERSITY PRESS®

25 24 23 22 1 2 3 4

CONTENTS

- 1 -

THE USE OF THOUGHTFORMS IN THE EXPANSION OF CONSCIOUSNESS

Mark L. Prophet

I think that we have to recognize the geometry of God, and the geometry of God is in the available thoughtforms—the trapezoid, the square, and the various symbols that have been used in some of the ancient fraternities. But we have to recognize that there is some validity in the use of these thoughtforms in the expansion of our consciousness. Now I'll try to show you how this works.

Down through the years we have had various dictations from the masters that relate to thoughtforms. One of the masters once said, for example, "You people have a consciousness about the size of a thimble when you should understand that you can expand it to the size of a barrel—or bigger."[1]

What are we doing but actually envisioning the hoop of the thimble, the circle itself, and the depth of the thimble—the size, the dimension of the thimble? And we are expanding it from the thimble to the barrel.

Basically, then, geometric forms can be utilized according to the size of familiar objects, and we can qualify them with greater dimension.

THE THOUGHTFORM OF A CUP

If we want to increase the capacity of our mind to receive, we can envision the thoughtform of a cup, a goblet, a chalice. The moment you think of a cup, you may have a tendency in your mind to associate the cup with a little cold water you're giving "in my name," you know, as Jesus said.[2] You think of the giving of something to someone else. So this in itself is an expansion or an extension of your own ideas, through the symbol of the cup, into the lives of others.

But let's change that cup now and put a base on it and make it into a chalice. Immediately you think

of the purification of the Holy Spirit, the descending dove coming down into the cup, you see. And you begin to feel that it is almost like a magnetic flux.

It's a flux of light—the bending of light rays into the cup to take the form of the cup. And when they bend in there, we suddenly get the idea of the accumulation of light rays—in other words, the laying of one light ray upon another, like a patine. You know how you take something and you will coat it with gold—gold-plate it? Well, that's overlaying or putting a patine of pure gold over our object.

In this case, we are going to cause light—which is descending from the Presence in the form of a dove—to bend in the chalice. And then it piles up, you see. The light rays just keep overlaying and overlaying and overlaying and finally they increase in density.

But of course, when you think of light, you think of illumination. So in reality you don't think of density, but still it is the density of light. But light doesn't have any density. You see, light has illumination. It has lumens. So we realize that we can cause light, mentally, to accumulate at a given spot.

The personal application and value of the use of thoughtforms in the expansion of consciousness relates to the human heart because the heart itself has within it a chamber—and it is a chamber of great beauty. And so we see that one can have chalices within chalices. One can have geometric forms within geometric forms.

COSMIC TRIGONOMETRY

Consciousness itself is actually constrained by thoughtforms. I want this understood by people.

It is both constrained, restrained, and expanded.

You can do a great deal with consciousness by creating thoughtforms that relate to the geometrizing of God. It's a sort of a cosmic trigonometry. It's a magnificent thing. It's a cosmic calculus. It's a form of the divine mind, being used for expansion purposes.

I think probably the idea that a human being contains enough "spaghetti" inside of him (if I may use the term "spaghetti" rather jokingly)—such as blood vessels and nerve paths and various other cylindrical networks, arterial cardiovascular networks, and nerve networks through the body—that if you took all these out of one human body and put them together, you would be able to go to the moon and more just on the length of these noodles that are inside of us.

So we have to recognize the ability of mentally compressing objects into a very small space. In a way we are a little jewel box, physically speaking. But we are also a little jewel box mentally.

We have a great deal more room in our jewel box from a mental standpoint than we do from a physical standpoint. But at the same time, when you involve yourself in the expansion of consciousness by thoughtforms, you have to recognize that the first step is to bring the thoughtform into consonance with your physical formation so that it becomes rational to you.

If you do not deal with a rational thoughtform, it's like going ahead and having a nebulous cloud out here in space. What is it but a cloud of steam? You try to define it. You try to name it. You try to duplicate it in thought and feeling and you cannot do it.

But, you see, when you deal with familiar objects such as your physical body, you can relate the fact that a thoughtform is being brought into your physical form. And then—by the power of the mind, which has the power of expansion—you can take it out of the body and put it anywhere you want in space.

Actually you are attracting to that thoughtform, then, the various emanations of your consciousness itself. You are creating an extension in consciousness which later becomes a method whereby you can expand your own mind and being.

TAKE DOMINION OVER YOUR LIFE

So you start out with a chalice. It's not very big. It's just a little cup or a glass around the heart. But you suddenly decide that you are going to begin to invoke the Spirit of God into that chalice. Well, someone may have some idea of the right and wrong of all this. They say, "What right do I have as an individual to invoke the Spirit of God into my chalice?"

You have every right because God gave it to you in the beginning. He said, "Let us make man in our image."[3] He made you in his image. He made you in his likeness. He created you to be the authority in your world.

The biggest problem today in all of the whole human race is the fact that people do not want to take authority in their world. Instead of taking authority in their world, they allow other people to literally push them around with different ideas.

Fads. Somebody over in Paris decided they're going to have long skirts, "maxiskirts," this year. So they go ahead and create the maxiskirt and the whole world, practically, follows the Paris fashion fad. And the same with the miniskirts and everything else.

So we have to understand that we have to take dominion over our life, and we have every right to do it in regard to these thoughtforms. You are then doing what God commanded you to do. He said, "Take dominion over the earth."[4] Well, he wasn't talking just about the physical earth. He was talking about the earth of yourself too.

What does it say in the Bible? It says, "And the earth standing in the water and out of the water."[5] What's it talking about—"In the water and out of the water"? It's talking about a human baptism, you see—someone standing in the water and out of the water.

THE GEOMETRIZING OF GOD

You have to understand that the geometrizing of God is the methodology of God. God has methods. If you look under a microscope very carefully, or if you study cytology and the makeup of the various cells of the body and different crystals of rocks and matter formations, you will realize that there is a natural geometry in the LORD's creation of the material of Matter itself. And "Matter" really means *Mater* (from the Latin), or "Mother." And, of course, our physicians have given this name to various parts of the body—like the *dura mater* of the brain and the *pia mater* and so on. So we have to understand all this.

Now here we are creating mentally a chalice around the heart. The value of that chalice is purely a starting value. It's valuable as a point where you can begin your expansion of consciousness. You can go out and suddenly decide you're going to drown yourself in a chalice so big that you can't even imagine it around yourself. But it has to be relevant to what you can imagine.

You cannot make an infinite chalice, now, can you—really? It has to be in the known universe. You have to deal with known objects. So you start out with the physical. You make your chalice bigger and bigger and bigger and bigger—and one of these days you come to the point where you can actually mentally decide that you're going to be within a chalice as big as the earth. And so you do just that!

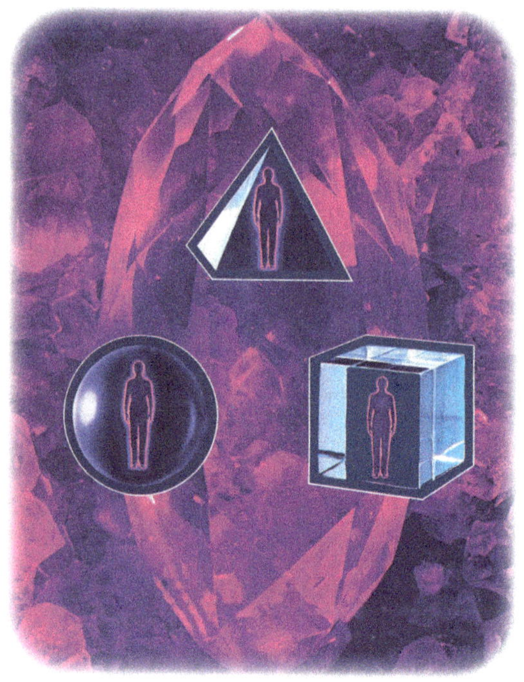

Now you may elect, instead of standing in a chalice, to stand in a pyramid or a cylinder or a square, a cube, or any other geometric object. And these thoughtforms can become the means of the expansion of your consciousness.

LIMIT YOUR EXPERIMENTS

I particularly want to warn the people that no one who is interested in tethering themselves to reality should indulge in this to the extent of more or less living in a world of fantasy or delusion. These should be controlled experiments in consciousness, and you should be careful to engage in them only for a limited period of time—because I'm going to tell you about the lever of relativity.

When you start these mental doings, you are starting a process in the Macrocosm that is occurring now first in the microcosm. You will not be able to create that infinite chalice we spoke about. But your God Presence can. And the pattern for these doings must, according to cosmic law, occur from your level. You have to be the authority for your world.

So by the creation of these proper thoughtforms and the endowment of yourself with the desire to produce these states of consciousness that are representative of an expanded awareness, you have to make these forms and then release them into the Universal.

I recommend and I advocate holy prayer before

doing so. I recommend protection from Mighty Astrea so that you are not in any way invaded by astral entities. I recommend care and consideration in the creation of these thoughtforms. And I recommend that after you have created them as large as you desire at a given time, that you then turn the thoughtform over to your God Presence for amplification.

Why? Because your God Presence has now received the mandate of your own authority to create. And whether you're awake or whether you're asleep or whether you're doing something else, your God Presence will take it up.

Do you know what that means—to "take it up"? Do you know the greatest healing that can occur in the whole world, for example, occurs when the God Presence does it? You in your human self can do nothing. When Jesus said, "I of myself can do nothing.... It is the Father in me which doeth the work,"[6] he was making the statement regarding the transfer of authority by the dominion of the human will to the divine will and the power of the cosmic lever of relativity acting for man in the name of God. Do you see?

It is an involved process, but I have tried to

reduce it to words that can be understandable by you. I personally have done a few things with this most effectively. And I know that it does work.

I suggest that you confine your early experiments of this nature to the more simple form because a great deal depends upon your own standards of morality, decency, and the elimination from your world of conflicting images. If you fill your mind with all of the crud (if I may use the word) of the world and then expect that you're going to start in and mix up this heavenly elixir with a human idea, it will not work as effectively. It may work a little, but I would be careful.

I would first try to purify the consciousness with the violet flame, I would have the highest motives in my doing, and I would make these determinations, and *then* I would work in the field of expanding my awareness and consciousness by the use of thoughtforms.

THE THOUGHTFORM OF WINGS

These thoughtforms also may include such objects as wings. I have spent a great deal of time with the thoughtform of wings. And I find that this is most valuable for elevating your consciousness.

In order to have wings, I suggest that you use Beethoven's Ninth Symphony, for example, or the Grail music from *Parsifal,* by Richard Wagner, or "The Ride of the Valkyries," or some of those high-quality classical renderings which are very inspiring and elevating to your consciousness. The *Lohengrin* music is also very good.

You use this music and then you envision a pair of wings, for example, on an hourglass, and you see the wings raising the hourglass. The idea is to elevate time into its proper use. And how better can you use it properly than to understand that God, who is eternity represented in the rising, is also magnetized, or drawn, into your image and then transferred to you—because you have the authority and because you have given that authority to your God Presence to act for you.

Without your mandate, without the mandate of prayer or the mandate of your decrees or the mandate of your desires in some manner voiced to the Spirit, there can be no manifestation. Basically, this is what was known long ago in some metaphysical movements as treasure mapping. But this is by far a more advanced method of doing it by dealing with geometric figures and thoughtforms.

Now, as I've said before, there are all kinds of thoughtforms that are valuable to pregnant mothers, for example. These thoughtforms are particularly valuable if they will try to trace mentally the lines of some of the great Grecian statues so that they can bring these lines into physical manifestation.

Roman copy of a Greek statue of Apollo

This is accomplished through first carrying the thoughtform up to their Christ Self and then to their God Presence—through their mandate, through their desire—and then calling for the perfect form to be brought down into their womb and utilized as the matrix which is then carried out by the body elemental of the mother and the formative elemental of the child.

WORKING WITH COLOR AND SOUND

Now I want to deal also with color in regard to our meditation. Let's say that we have created this chalice colorless. We've created it in black and white. It is possible for us to embellish the thoughtform by the use of correct color, primarily pastel colors such as the beautiful pinks, the beautiful violets, the beautiful soft pastel yellows. All of these colors actually can be drawn mentally within the object of our thoughtform.

You may say to me, "Well wouldn't the black and white be enough?" No. Because the black and white in reality is to a certain degree involved with the nature of the gray ones. While the white is all right, the moment you put any black into it at all, you are going to dilute your whole situation. You'll dilute the whole formula, you see. So I suggest that rather than use black, you use colors. Even in the formation of what you would consider to be the black and white lines that make up the form of the chalice, I would suggest that you actually use color rather than use black as the demarcation line for your subject.

I want to bring in another factor here which is extremely important in the use of thoughtforms, and that is the quality of tone. Now after you've created, we'll say, a beautiful violet-colored chalice in the ethers, involving either the heart or the heart chakra or even the third eye or any other part of your being, you can qualify that with tone. And by "tone" I mean you can cause the object itself to appear as an object of pink glass, as though you took a metal rod and caused the glass to vibrate so that it will emit a tone.

In other words, we are endowing our thought creation with the quality of a solid object, and we are giving it the quality of creating a musical tone. Do you see what I mean? You can do this with any object having a geometric form.

Now it is always desirable that we call for such a tone as the high C vibration, for example. The idea is that if we get the right tone, it will vibrate according to certain laws of the universe and actually produce a physical manifestation.

This science of *intonation* is a part of the "hidden wisdom" spoken of by Paul as the mystery of God.[7] So I'm not permitted to give you the full structure of what you can do with tone in connection with the mind. But I can say that in this mental picture you can use tone, which gives a further solidity to your object from a mental standpoint.

Whatever you send out will return to you. So by this law, if you don't use the quality of a tone in your thought creation, you are going to lack something of value to yourself.

The more reality you can put into the mental image, the greater chances you have of this object materializing—not necessarily in the sense that you're going to bring forth beautiful little glasses that are going to drop from the Universal, as Baird Spalding described.[8] (This happens to be one of the steps, however.) But I'm talking about improving and expanding awareness and consciousness through guiding your thoughts along these geometric lines, which is one of the first steps that you're going to have to take before you can use the creative abilities that God has given you.

Later on you can use this in symmetry such as the molding of sculpture. You can actually mold and sculpt, if you wish, using these principles. But I think that the person who begins to work first in the realm of mind and form and cosmic symmetry has a better chance of executing this in the world of form than the person who does not.

INCREASE YOUR CREATIVE ABILITIES

I recommend to all of you who are interested in these experiments that you engage in them for a limited time rather than a maximum time. If you do engage in them a maximum time, you may find that you will be subject to potentially harmful influences. But by using them just for a short time, like five minutes once or twice a day, you'll begin to condition your mind and your spirit and your being to your creative abilities.

And these creative abilities will come out in all of your work. You will begin to understand how to use your physical senses in an improved manner. You will understand that you are working with the fingers of the mind and with the creative ability of the mind through the use of these thoughtforms, and later you will transfer your sensory awareness to your fingertips.

This means that you will be able to have an expanded awareness in your lower consciousness (as well as in your higher consciousness) and increased sensitivity in your analyses of conditions and things and people.

You will find that you can, with greater ease, pick up on vibratory patterns and that you will be less subject to the mental manipulations of various people who are using witchcraft and various forms of black magic against you, for example, or against anyone in the world, because you will be stronger for using these images. Through the creation of these thoughtforms under God's direction, through your I AM Presence, you will find that you will have greater control of your creative aspects than you have ever had before.

Now don't expect this control to manifest immediately. It may not do so for a period of three or four months. But if you keep building into your consciousness your valuable experiments in the use of thoughtforms for the expansion of consciousness—purely for the use of good—you will be strengthening your mental body and your creative faculties.

I recommend to you then that you try this—but don't make it a god to yourself. This is only one of the creative aspects of life. There are many.

AVOID CONDEMNATION

So now you are dealing with a tone, you're dealing with a color. In our recognition of the use of these creative faculties, a great deal is to be obtained. Man is actually preparing to enter into his own divinity. In reality he was made in the divine image. This is one way he can return to that pure image.

What a silly thing that people are stressing all of this "in sin did my mother conceive me."[9] Well, condemnation really is a tool of the forces of evil and it is not to be used by the spiritual aspirant on the spiritual path. He should not use it against others or against himself. Condemnation is stultifying. It prevents a man from actually realizing what things are all about—what is real about himself and what is illusory.

So I think maybe, just out of the interest of further enhancing your creative ability, I will give you a little skit that I sometimes do for the benefit of some people. They'll come up to me and they'll ask me a question and they'll say, "Do you know this?" or "Do you know that?"

And I'll say, "Well, not knowing with any great degree of certainty, I therefore hesitate to respond to you, fearing that I might thereby prevaricate and suffer dire calamity, which has naught to do with the indubitable angelic acclamation of the ineffable austerity of the approaching woes, or the incontrovertible inexhaustibility of divine providence. By now I hope that your sufficiency is quite suffancified because any more'd be a vulgar superfluity."

This is the sort of thing that really doesn't do anything for you but it probably entertains you a little bit.

THE USE OF THE SPIRAL

So I want to bring to your attention that creative ability is possible through the use of geometric figures. And I also want to take up the spiral because this is a delightful mechanism.

We are dealing now with the circle, or the laws of eternal cycles. We can create a golden cycle. And then we can attach this cycle mentally to the next cycle. The way to do it is with the spiral—then you have a natural flow, you see. You have no interruption if you do it with circles.

Can you imagine piling circles one on top of each other like a bunch of dinner plates? You begin to wonder, after a while, if they're all going to fall down. So instead of that you just connect them in one beautiful flow and it's a spiral staircase that leads to the stars!

Well, you know, you would be absolutely amazed when you begin working with these figures to realize that God used geometry so wonderfully to illustrate to humanity their own natural abilities to scale the stars in creative thought—because this is very practical. Through these exercises, uneducated men can suddenly become educated. Why? Because we are dealing with the automation processes.

I think most of you are familiar with the Russian scientist Pavlov and the "conditioned reflexes." It was a matter of placing sensing devices in the mouth of a dog to register the saliva. Pavlov found that by ringing a dinner bell and then feeding the dog he could measure the saliva that would always come whenever the dog would be fed. Well, later on he took away the food and rang the bell and he still got the saliva. So he began to understand the matter of conditioned responses, you see.

Now unfortunately, the Pavlovian theories have been used in a negative way by Lavrentiy Beria, who used to be with the NKVD, or the Soviet secret police. They used it in a wrong way as a hypnotic device to manipulate and control political prisoners in times of war and to influence people in various nations where they could use these principles against them. But this was a very limited thing.

That was only a first step for man to understand the spirals of the cosmos and the controls that can be actually used by us for our betterment—to help ourselves and also to guard against the influences of other people who have nefarious ideas, who don't yet understand the principles that God has given us of "live and let live."

We have no right to try to influence anybody else against their free will. God doesn't practice it, does he? But we have every intent of practicing for ourselves the taking of dominion over our world and the developing of our own creative ability.

If we don't develop it, somebody else isn't going to develop it for us—are they? Do you believe they are? They can't, can they? It's impossible. We have to develop it for ourselves. Each of you will have to follow these experiments.

It's like the dead language of Latin, for example. You have a Latin scholar and you have the Latin scholar go ahead and learn to speak Latin. Well, you say, "It's a dead language. Who wants to speak

Latin?" But the mental gymnastics involved in the speaking of Latin prepare him for the understanding of almost every other language on the face of the earth, and they give him the ability to think properly.

I think we should understand the need to make ourselves do these things just the same as we eat our daily bread. We've got to become a well-rounded person, a person that is able to utilize the mechanics of the Spirit in the creating of form.

I happen to believe that even when you come to the point of your ascension and you come to the point where you have risen to be, more or less, a god —did you hear what I said? I said a *god*—you. Yes, you. That's who I'm talking to. As the Psalmist said, "Ye are gods."[10] Somewhere along the pathway, if you're going to be "children of the Most High," you've got to master all of these things that deal with the control and creation of form and substance.

And form and substance is very important to Spirit. Because Spirit created it for a reason. There is a raison d'être, you see, to the creation of substance. And actually what we're trying to do with these thoughtforms is to give you a creative power and a control of your own life and your life energies.

It's a pantomime that eventually will become a very effective means of helping you to grow spiritually. Yes, it could be used negatively. But if you do, you'll pay and pay and pay. So I pray to God that nobody will ever use it in a negative way, but just use this knowledge to try to take your first toddling steps in dealing with energy from a higher level.

God bless you and thank you for your attention.

- 2 -

PLUS IS GREATER

Mark L. Prophet

> *He that believeth on me, the works that I do shall he do also; and greater works than these shall he do; because I go unto my Father.*
>
> —JESUS CHRIST

Mankind at one point or another receives from God self-individualization. It is the flame at the heart of the atom. It is the nucleus of our life. It is the *summum bonum* of our identity at the inner core of being. With this endowment of individualization from the Godhead, you have life and consciousness—awareness of life.

As you begin to live, you act and you also think. And hopefully, one of your acts is the act of determination.

You make a determination that you ought to do a certain thing. And when you do it, your act—at first no more than a motive—now becomes crystallized as a part of your own personal recorded history.

If that act that you perform is beneficial, if it is helpful to others, if it contributes to the universe, then you have fulfilled the words that the Lord described in the parable—you have added unto yourself, or added unto life, a plus factor. And that plus factor helps the universe grow with you.

POSITIONING IN THE PYRAMID OF LIFE

Now, if you were to take a handkerchief out of your pocket and hold that handkerchief before you, and then poke it right in the center and then put your fingers around it and pull it down, you would notice that you have an apex to that handkerchief. That apex is like the apex of a pyramid. It's the highest point, or summit, of that pyramid's achievement.

From an individualized standpoint, we are positioned in life according to whether our acts, our feelings, and our conduct place us at the base of the pyramid or down here even below the base in the subterranean strata of the pyramid. Somewhere we are positioned on that ladder of consciousness, or ladder of life.

If we perform an act that is positive, that adds to the betterment of life, as we perform this act—I don't care if it's only a one one-hundredth or one one-thousandth of an inch—it will make that whole structure rise.

Everybody that does anything constructive in this universe raises this total symbolic picturing of the total being of man. We all go up! And if somebody does something that is negative, it has a tendency to create a drag on the consciousness. Why? Because all rise is in consciousness. Consciousness precedes the crystallization of substance, of acts. In other words, actions must crystallize into the path.

You start out first with a thought. And the thought at the time that you act is the path—because now it is an act, not a thought. And after a while, it is only a memory.

The thoughts, the acts, and the memory constitute various parts of a flow. The flow is a chain. Act one of this chain will be motivation and thought. Act two will be the action. Act three is the memory.

LIVING IN THE ETERNAL NOW

We can use an hourglass to illustrate this point. We can say that the sand in the top of the hourglass represents our potential—your potential and my potential. There is a nexus in the hourglass and the sand falls through that nexus—the sand of potential. And when it passes through, it is an act and you realize it.

Now then, when you come to the point where the sand is at the bottom of the glass, you have nothing but memory—that is, the memory of what took place. That's why they say most of us live in the eternal now. We live in the eternal now—that's the sense we have of what is passing through the nexus of the hourglass now.

We live in a sense of time as a moving activity. And we ourselves actually swim through the time belt. But it is possible for a man or a woman or a child to go through this time belt and nothing happens.

THE PARABLE OF THE POUNDS

This is why Jesus Christ used the parable of the pounds when he was speaking to some people who were of the opinion that the kingdom of God would appear immediately, you see, now that the Messiah had come.

In this parable, Jesus talks about a nobleman who was preparing for a journey to a faraway country to receive for himself a kingdom. Before he left, the nobleman gave to his ten servants ten pounds—one each. And he said, "Occupy till I come."[1]

Now, when the nobleman returned he called those ten servants to find out how much they had gained "by trading." One servant came and said, "Lord, thy pound gained ten pounds." Plus is greater.

He added to the one pound that he was given by God ten more pounds. And the Lord in return gave him authority over ten cities.

Then we find the wicked servant taking out his napkin, putting in his one pound, and carefully folding up the napkin. Now the Lord comes back—and the servant is trembling because he knows how great the Lord is. He takes out his napkin, unfolds it, looks his Lord in the eye (and you wonder how he dared!) and says, "Here is the pound thou gavest me. I've laid it up in a napkin and carefully preserved it because I knew you were a hard man. I knew you were austere. I knew your laws were tough. I knew you were very exacting. I knew you wanted A students not C students. So I have taken awfully good care of what you gave me and I haven't lost a jot or tittle of it. Here it is. I'm not giving the universe anything back—but I'm not taking anything away from the universe, Lord. So please be merciful to me."

The Lord looked at him and leaned over backwards a little bit. And he said, "Out of thy own mouth I will judge thee, thou wicked servant. Thou knewest I was an austere man. Why didn't you put my money into the bank so that I could have it back now with interest." And the nobleman said to the other servants, "Take this man's pound and give it to that one over there who had ten pounds."

"Unto every one which hath shall be given; and from him that hath not, even that he hath shall be taken away."[2]

THE LESSON OF PLUS IS GREATER

Now in this parable of the pounds we learn that plus is greater. The *plus* factor is a very important factor to every one of you because it concerns your life and your identity. It concerns your future.

You can go through life, if you wish, and say to the universe, "You're a bank. And every time I can, I'm going to rob you." That is what people do. They think that the universe owes them a living. I'm not talking about your daily bread and those things. I'm talking about the fact that some people think that because they were created by God and endowed with opportunity that they ought to be taken care of.

In other words, God ought to provide some

kind of a relief system for them so they wouldn't have to work. All they'd have to do is go through life and collect their manna from heaven every day. It should descend on them from heaven and just carry them through. And everybody else should be blessed by that and should imitate them. What a travesty this is—as an idea.

I quote from Jesus Christ: "My Father worketh hitherto, and I work."[3] The universe needs to have the plus factor fed into it. You and I are never more than anyone else. But our deeds can be. The difference between people upon this planet is solely one of deeds and correct action and correct thought.

THE PATH TO BECOMING GOD

I don't care whether you believe in Buddha or Christ or just believe in God or what you believe—it doesn't make any difference. I'm stating a law. You can call God any name you want to, he's still Christ. Both God and Christ belong to man, and they are the spiritual instruments by which man is raised above the level of the animal.

You are not an animal. You are intended to be

a god—and today you probably are an embryonic god in the making.

The experiences you have are intended to clarify in your consciousness what things are of value to you for the spiritual journey and what things are of harm. So when I say that plus is greater, I mean that it is better to add to yourself a constructive act all the day long than it is to add the lukewarmness of just vegetating or idling the mind and consciousness.

Learning and instruction are for your profit, that you might gain spiritually. But I think it is a gross error that individuals may think in terms of personal growth at the sacrifice of the universe. The universe needs you and you and you—it needs us all! And it needs us as constructive spiritual masons and architects of the New Age.

We can understand that God drew the blueprint of the square at the base of the pyramid. We can understand that he put the star at the top of Christhood and the plumb line from that star to the center of our square. But it is up to us to build and to construct these lively stones of our lives into a monumental achievement that may be enshrined by the fires of God and crowned by the capstone thereof to shine in not only the desert places of life but throughout the tabernacle of the whole world.

PROBLEMS WITH PLUS IS GREATER

There are certain problems that are inherent within the concept of "plus is greater." Let me give you some of these problems.

Boredom. "I am alone. Just me and nobody else. Nobody else can look in the mirror through my eyes. I'm alone." How true. But how universal.

We are all alone. But spell it this way, a-l-l-o-n-e, and it makes "all one." What it really means is we'll all win together.

In a sense, we are on that bobsled going downhill. And if we drag our feet, that bobsled is going to slow down. And if we all keep our feet up on the bobsled, we'll get there faster.

Now there are people that enjoy dragging the bobsled. They like to create problems and maladies for others because they don't think the universe is really fair. They think that life is rigged. They either know or don't know about their karmic record and so they say to themselves, "Well, I've had a hard time. All my life, I've had a hard time."

The concept of doom and gloom and all of this stuff that goes with it is the result of people's failures to recognize that plus is greater. And so, they are a big minus mark and wherever they go they subtract from the universe. That's what makes a man greedy and hoardy. Why, they would hoard

God if they knew how to put him together as a commodity. And they'd put him away in a stocking somewhere and bury it in the heart of the earth. That's a wrong concept.

Begin to look at your life as though it were a beautiful sack just chock-full of goodies—because it is. You begin to bring those goodies out of that sack like your own Santa Claus. And it will be so. You decide that you're going to not just give these goodies to yourself, but you're going to share these goodies with everybody on earth.

Each person should work with their own hands that they may have to give to those that need, said Saint Paul.[4] This means that each one of us should take the hands of divine opportunity that have been given to us and put them to work in a practical manner that we may enjoy an abundance of every good thing as God intended from the beginning.

CREATING THE PLUS CONSCIOUSNESS

A plus consciousness is one that is always acquiring something with the talents we have. If you will just put your consciousness to work at any age acquiring something—it doesn't have to be money, it doesn't have to be reading material, it doesn't have to be, but it can be any of these things; it could be crocheting that you're giving away to people at Christmas; it can be anything, you name it—it's a plus. It can be the acquisition of spiritual peace. It can be the acquisition of any of your talents. Whatever it is, is between you and God.

All of us have to recognize that we face every day as a fresh new page, right from the hand of God. He made that page. You write on it, by your actions and your thoughts. Your thoughts precede your actions.

Getting back, then, to the fact that plus is greater (which is the thing I want to leave with you), the plus consciousness is the greatest consciousness. And now I'm going to say something I don't want you to forget—and that is that you and your consciousness are one. You are basically your consciousness, because no matter how great the matrix of God is (and it's very great!), if your mind is a thimble and God is a waterfall of infinite light, you can only hold a thimbleful. Just remember that. But if you enlarge that thimble to be a barrel, you've caught an awful lot more of God.

PUTTING THE PLUS FACTOR TO WORK

So plus is greater. And, in reality, if our consciousness can become an educated consciousness aware of the opportunities we have for service (p.s., that means work!)—if we'll put ourselves to work for God, the plus factor of our life will carry us all the way Home.

Well, how are we going to do it? We're going to do it by putting that thimble into a barrel and the barrel into a bigger barrel until after a while we can hold enough of God that we won't have to worry whether or not we're going to cope with the world's problems. There is no problem God cannot solve. There is no problem that plus cannot solve.

So the power of positive thinking and the power of positive feeling and the power of positive regeneration—this can give us a different and right attitude toward life. And with that right attitude, we will win the fight. We will win the game instead of being a pawn that everybody pushes around, and after a while we say, "Move me off the board! I don't want to fight any longer."

Don't feel that way. Don't feel that no one cares, that no one loves you. Someone does. But the problem is, you've left out of that thimble of consciousness the knowledge of how much He loves you. It may be in every drop of water that falls into the thimble, but God is so big that there's only a minute dilution of each of his qualities in every drop. So sometimes it helps if you just get a little more quantity in order to enhance your quality. Do you see what I mean?

Get a little more of God so you can see a sample in larger proportion of every quality he has. As Thomas à Kempis said, "Imitate Christ."

As we learn to imitate him in our thoughts and our feelings, as we learn to have a plus-is-greater consciousness, as we learn to *be* a plus-is-greater consciousness, our world itself will take on those aspects. It'll keep getting better and better and better.

The Chart of Your Divine Self

- 3 -

THE CHART OF YOUR REAL SELF— THE HIGHEST THOUGHTFORM

Mark L. Prophet

The Chart itself is a very marvelous compilation of man's true reality. It shows you your own relationship to God. If this Chart could have been in the hands of the Christian Church and understood early in this century, we would have an entirely different world today because it gives a scientific explanation of man's individual relationship to God.

Quite a few years ago, I heard someone say to another person, "Who in the world do you think you are? Do you think you're God or something?" No doubt, you have discovered that this is possible, that people will say these things to one another. Is that bad?

Well, it must be terrible because Jesus was practically pushed over the brink of a hill because he called himself the Son of God.[1] People are very touchy about their Gods, whether they have just one or many. And they don't like anyone to claim that they are God.

One of the tricks of the evil forces on the planet is what is known as intimidation. They intimidate you through inferiority. They try to make you feel so small and so insignificant and so little that you figure, "Well, I haven't got a chance to run in this race anyway. I might as well quit before I start."

The Chart is the most immaculate proof of the fact that you do have a chance—because there isn't a man or a woman or a child upon this planet whom God created that does not have this exact relationship to him. This does not deny Jesus, it affirms him. But it affirms Jesus, or the Christ, within the range of your touch. It makes it possible for you to reach him and to have a personal relationship with him, and through him with God. And it's a lot different than you may realize at this point.

THE GOD PRESENCE

The upper figure in the Chart is the individualized God Presence of each one of you and of each one of us. Let us understand, then, that man has been confused by his own time-spatial relationship. How many angels can dance on the head of a pin? An infinite number, because angels do not displace time or space.

But somehow or other we can't get through our heads the idea of walking through one another. If we get into a revolving door and there is someone else in there with us, somebody might get hurt. So when it comes to spatial relationships, we realize that two people can't occupy the same square foot at the same time. It's just impossible.

So we have a little difficulty in fixing, "Where is God?" Where, indeed? He's everywhere. Well, this doesn't quite satisfy a child. And somehow or other, even man is not quite satisfied with it. We always have the idea that God should be somewhere and that maybe if we go to him, we could find him.

That's why Jesus said that "false Christs and

false prophets shall arise, saying, Christ is here and Christ is there; but go not. . . . For the kingdom of heaven is within you."[2] Now let us see what he meant.

He meant that within every one of you, God's kingdom was already. He meant that it is not blasphemy for you to think of yourself as in the image of God—because God created you in his image. So what's wrong in thinking that you're in his image?

Physically speaking, your body may not look just like God's body. But you're not your body any more than you are your dress or your suit of clothes or your overcoat. Your body is something you wear. It may fit you like a glove, or you may think it does. But you may find out that it doesn't fit you so well when you find out what you really look like. Because this upper figure in the Chart, which we call your I AM God Presence, is being, is yours. It belongs to you.

THE IMAGE OF GOD

There is one magnificent, eternal, divine God Presence in the Great Central Sun who has the nature of the one God, which is to be androgynous, and is called Alpha and Omega. Jesus said in Revelation, "I AM Alpha and Omega, the beginning and the ending."[3] Therefore, the beginning and the ending of every man and of all creation is God. However, this God in the heart of the Great Central Sun has the power to duplicate his image and make as many luminous presences of himself as he wishes.

It's just like a woman who has a whole pile of dough and rolls it out with a rolling pin and she gets a cookie cutter out. She can have a cookie cutter that looks like a gingerbread man. She can stamp out as many cookies as she wants to, and they all look alike.

So don't expect you're going to find anything different between your I AM Presence and mine. Jesus' I AM Presence looks just like yours. This is the common denominator. God created all men equal. But he created you equal only in the sense that he gave you an I AM Presence, he gave you a Divine Self.

Many people have looked up to heaven. And

when they looked up to heaven, they've seen their God Presence and they thought they saw an angel. Because your Presence is very radiant and very beautiful. And around your Presence are concentric rings of great power. Here is where people begin to differ in their Divine Self.

You have an I AM Presence, and it looks just like everybody else's, it looks just like God's. You can't say that a man is more God, or that God is more God than himself, or that man is less God. If God created man in his own image, he made him in his own image period. There are no differences.

We have to understand this in order to understand the Chart, because we have to change our thinking. We can't keep thinking that we're just nothing, because nothing could not possibly come forth from nothing, could it? Therefore, something came forth from something. And what came forth, of course, is the divine man—divine *man*ifestation.

Oh, he doesn't look very divine now, does he, when you see him lying drunk in the gutter? When you see him out here misbehaving, committing mayhem and murder and all kinds of things, he doesn't look very divine. But upstairs he is. Up here, everybody is divine. There is absolutely no difference.

THE CAUSAL BODY

But here is where the difference comes in, and this is important. In the Bible it says, "One star differeth from another star in glory. So also is the resurrection of the dead."[4] This means, that people have different sized causal bodies—the color bands around the I AM Presence. These are spheres of energy—pulsating energy, permanent energy, eternal energy. They are spiritual light energy, and each band has a different color.

For example, the white has all the colors of the rainbow in it. It's a symbol of purity. Every time that you permit purity to function in your world, every time you perform any ablution, whether you're washing your hands or whatever you're doing, that is adding to the size of that band of white. And every single thing that you do to keep yourself pure is yours forever.

You can't ever lose what you gain spiritually. And you gain spiritually, physically, as well as otherwise. Everything that you do for purification adds to the size of this white band. And the bigger it gets, the more purity you have in your world. That's why one star differs from another star in glory.

The yellow is symbolic of wisdom. Every time you pick up the scriptures and you read or you study, every time you learn any new thing, you add to your storehouse of knowledge. And that adds to the size of the golden sphere of illumination in your causal body.

You know what that causal body is? It's laying up "treasures in heaven, where," Jesus said, "thieves cannot break through and steal, and moths cannot eat, or rust consume."[5] Everything that you do where God works through you of purity, of learning, or of expressing love, as in this pink band, every time you're loving and kind to any human being, immutably, *immutably*—the Law demands it—it registers up there by God's I AM.

Whatever you do of good down here in the human end, the physical form, is registered up there in your causal body. That's why you never lose it. You can lose your body. You can even lose your mind. But you *never* will lose your causal body. It's there forever.

What's the violet band? That's the quality of mercy that "is not strain'd. It droppeth as the gentle rain from heaven upon the place beneath: it is twice blest; it blesseth him that gives and him that takes."[6] That's mercy and forgiveness.

The purple sphere is the power of transmutation and diplomacy.

And here is the green sphere. Green represents the folding stuff you carry in your wallets—abundance. It is also chlorophyll, the green of nature. It's the healing power of the universe. It's a combination of the yellow and the blue, isn't it? It's the wisdom and the power to produce good health. That's in the green sphere. That's why many physicians in their operating rooms today are wearing green, because that color is health. Chlorophyll—imprisoned splendor of the sun.

And what's that blue circle? That's power. That's the first ray. That's the will of God. That's faith. Every time you have faith in divine things, you add to the size of that sphere.

So this is your causal body, or your heavenly storehouse, it's your cosmic bank. And every single one of you has a different sized causal body. If you're really wise, you're really smart, you probably have a lot of yellow in your causal body. If you're really full of power, you have a lot of faith, you will have a lot of blue. If you're in the healing arts, or you're a banker, you probably have a lot of green.

THE SILVER CORD

How does the energy of the causal body, which is your cosmic bank, get down here into the human? It comes down through this silver cord. Probably some of you remember that song, "The silver cord is loosened and the golden bowl is broken."[7] Well, the golden bowl is the protective light that abides around the physical heart. It's not a part of the physical heart, but is actually the spiritual light that comes down around the heart.

And when a baby is born, that little baby's head has a cleft in it where the bone is left open. Most people don't know why that is. The reason for that is so that this silver cord can come down through the top of the head, anchor down in the heart and start the pulsation, the impulse of the heart and make it beat.

Therefore, as long as you live, wherever you walk in a sense of the word, just like a little girl running through a park with a big balloon and a string going up, you are dangled right below your own causal body and your own I AM Presence. There is a silver cord running down right through your head down to your heart, and that's what beats your heart. And it goes with you everywhere you go, just like Mary's little lamb.

I know some of these idioms may seem foolish, but I'm trying to help you remember. I want you to remember. And after a while you'll learn to use other language.

THE TUBE OF LIGHT

Now what is this white cylinder in the Chart? That is the tube of light. The tube of light can only be invoked from your God Presence, your own divine I AM Presence, your great source. It is the natural protection that a man needs today to move in the world of form without suffering the invasion into his world of mental problems, of entities, of states of unhappiness, of anger, of resentment, of jealousy, of discord.

Some of you may not believe this at first. But a person who is jealous can walk past you on the bus and touch your shoulder, and if your tube of light is not on you or you don't have a naturally strong protection, you can pick up that jealousy and it will go right through you. And if you are exposed to a jealous situation, that jealousy you picked up from the other person will be residual in your world and it will act.

So the tube of light is your great crystal-light overcoat of protection that you can put all around you. I've told you at times a story about how one of our students in Washington, D.C., got hit by a car. There was a loud shattering noise. And when this happened, the driver got out and he said, "Are you hurt?" And the student said, "No, you never touched me; you just touched my tube of light."

Everyone laughed. But at the same time, we find that some of the masters in India have a tube of light that is so hard, it's so strong and so tangible, that they have let people shoot an elephant gun at them. The bullet would come to the tube of light, about six feet from their body, and it was flattened and dropped right down to the ground. I know it might sound like a fairy tale to you. It isn't. But

I don't advise the average person to try it.

This tube of light can be invoked. And when you want to have the tube of light come down, you call for it. If I invoked the tube of light, you'd feel it out there in the audience. And I'm sure that I'd feel it too if some of you invoked it. And the more you invoke the tube of light every day, calling two or three times a day for that tube to be put around you, the more you become conscious of that tube, the more it becomes a reality around you.

The greatest protection you can have is that tube of light. And you've got to build it. In one sense of the word, I can compare that tube of light to the wedding garment that Jesus talked about. He said there was a certain feast and the people came with their wedding garment on. There was one man there and he didn't have any wedding garment on. The master walked up to him and he said, "Where is your wedding garment?" He said, "Take him and cast him into outer darkness, where there is weeping and gnashing of teeth."[8]

Well that sounded terrible. When I read it the first time, I thought, "My, the Lord is very firm, isn't he?" Well, he is firm, because he was stating the Law. And the Law is that if you don't have the wedding garment or the tube of light on, you're going to be in outer darkness anyway. And if you're in outer darkness, you're there, aren't you? And you are going to gnash your teeth because you will have a lot of things you can't handle. You can handle a lot more with your tube of light.

But it's like the old sinner who said, "I became a saint and I'm saved, but now I backslid." You can tear a hole in your garment by anger, by viciousness, by fear. You can rend your own garment. And when you do, you have to call on the law of forgiveness and ask God to forgive you for it, and then you have to rebuild it again. You patch it up. And light patches very easily and it gets very strong again. So don't neglect putting that garment on every day.

Some people have the idea that it doesn't amount to much. It amounts to a lot. I'll try to give you an illustration of the difference it makes.

If you were to go into a room where you're a stranger, a Baptist convention, and everybody there knew that you happened to be a follower of the ascended masters. The organization, because it believes in reembodiment, would not be popular with the Baptists. These people could turn on you, and they could think a lot of things. They might say, "Oh here's one of them. And the Bible says I shouldn't even eat with these people, because they don't believe the same as I do. So I'll give them the cold shoulder"—that's a nice interpretation of what they might think.

So they start sending all those arrows of hostility. Do you know what Shakespeare called them? "The slings and arrows of outrageous fortune."[9] So these slings and arrows of outrageous fortune are coming against you. When they hit your tube of light, they don't come through, and you don't feel it at all.

I happened to be present one time in a church when the minister told the people that I was the devil. And at that precise moment, when he stood there in the pulpit leveling all the denunciations of hell on my head, that tube of light was lowered before I knew there was a tube of light.

God lowered that tube of light and I saw it.

It dropped right down around me, and I couldn't even hear his voice anymore. It got so strong that his voice faded away and it sounded like a muffled tone coming through a big set of double doors. And there I was, the happiest thing you ever saw. So it works.

THE CHRIST SELF

Anchored midway between your divine God Presence, the I AM of you, which is individualized and makes you equal with every other human being on earth, and your lower self, right in between, the pivot point of it all, is the Christ.

The Christ is not Jesus, per se—although he, himself, certainly became the Christ. The Christ means *Christos,* or the light by which God made all things. It is also known as the Word, or the *Logos.* The Logos was the Word that went forth, by which all things were made.[10]

When the Logos spoke through Jesus, the Logos said, "Before Abraham was, I AM."[11] You can say the same thing and it will be true of you, too. Because the I AM was, the divine being existed long

before our flesh form in any of our embodiments. And the I AM will continue to exist.

The I AM is not the soul. Some people have the idea that the I AM is the soul. I would say you could call it the Spirit, because there's only one Spirit, and we all have a little of it in us.

Take the Pacific Ocean. It's pretty big, isn't it? Take one drop out of it. That's you. You're just a drop of water out of the ocean. You have every single quality of the whole ocean in that drop—quality, I said, but not quantity. The only way you get the quantity is to be like the salt doll, to dissolve yourself in the ocean. And what you can do, every master does.

When a master heals a man who is sick, he merges himself with the ocean. And in that merging, all the power in the universe flows through him. That's why in that dominant state of Christ consciousness, Jesus said, "All power is given unto me in heaven and in earth."[12]

That is the signative claim. You lay hold on eternal life. You claim it for yourself. It already is yours, but the Law requires that you claim it. You have to demand it for yourself. And you'll never get it, dear hearts, never in all of this world, if you don't demand it.

The dark force of the planet will put you down

every time. They'll try to keep you away. They'll tell you that you're not very smart. They'll tell you that you're not very important. You're just as important as any other human being. And if there ever was an intimidating thought or concept, it's this idea of making you feel unimportant so that you'll turn around and do everything in your power to show other people how important you really are, thus wasting your energy on the human self and losing your divine inheritance.

You've already got God. You couldn't have anything higher. You got just as much of God as anyone else has. But everyone has opportunity to build this causal body bigger and bigger.

THE PARACLETE

The dove is symbolical of the Paraclete, the Holy Spirit. It is an interesting thing that the Holy Spirit is a tangible manifestation. And while there are only a few churches today that stress the Holy Spirit, it is a very important thing in the plan of God. But there really isn't too much point in receiving the Holy Spirit if you don't keep it. If you get it, you should keep it—otherwise, what's the use of getting it? You just make yourself more accountable.

Therefore, I stress that the Holy Spirit should be retained. And the way to retain it is to keep your character in the same state of consciousness as God himself.

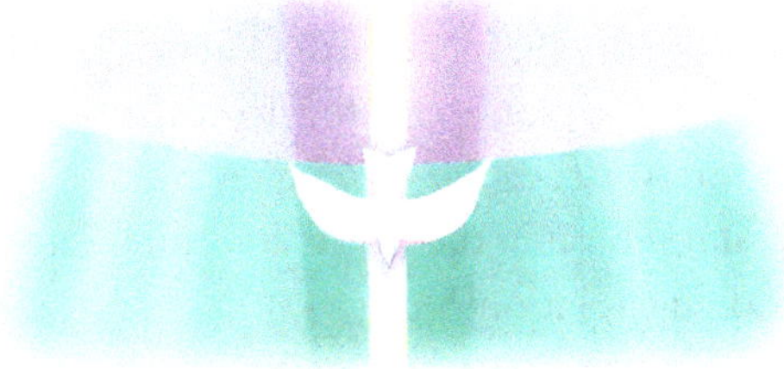

Do you remember that minister by name of Charles Sheldon, who wrote *In His Steps?* The pastor in the story had a little card he put on his desk, and it said, "What would Jesus do?" And every single decision he had to make, he looked at that card and asked himself that question.

That's building divine character. You don't ask yourself, "What would I do?" but "What would Jesus do?" And then do what he would do. You really have to build his character. And the Holy

Spirit, when it comes in, comes through the Christ consciousness down into the chalice of man.

THE LOWER FIGURE

Notice how the hands of the lower figure, the supplicant, are raised up. That's because man really hungers for God and wants him. A lot of people today are glorying in atheism. They say, "God is dead." But did you ever stop to realize just how much interest there is in religion today? It's the most vital subject in the world. So man is interested in his divine relationship.

This human down here exists in order to bring this I AM Presence down to his level. There's only one reason why you're on earth, and that is to master your world. And there's only one way you can master your world, and that's by letting God live in you. But the Christ acts as the Mediator between God and man. The universal Christ becomes identified at the midpoint between man and God. Do you know why this is so?

Because God is so innocent that he doesn't even know that evil exists. And you won't either when

you get into his state of completeness. God is that innocent. His eyes are too pure to behold iniquity.[13] Therefore, the Presence is absolutely unaware of any evil anywhere. In one sense, then, God doesn't actually know that you're sick. He only knows that he made you well. You know what I mean?

Therefore, the Christ must be invoked. The

Christ possesses the simultaneous power of knowing the perfection of God and also knowing the needs of man. That's why there is nothing that equals the Christ—the Christ can really bring you to God.

When you ascend, where do you ascend to? You ascend into the Christ, and the Christ ascends back to the Father. That is the way it's done. Therefore, when God says, "Draw nigh unto me and I will draw nigh unto you,"[14] he means it.

And I want to point out to everyone in this room that for an atheist, this human figure in the Chart is down here and his Presence is probably seventy feet up in the air—roughly speaking. I want to point out to you that for a student of the ascended masters, the Presence may be only nine or ten feet above your head—because, "Draw nigh unto me and I will draw nigh unto you."

In the advanced chela, the Holy Christ Self can come down and envelop him. You can reach a point where you can draw the Christ around yourself until he actually frames your image. You can so change your countenance that it will be altered. And just like Peter and James and John on the mountaintop,[15] people will meet you when you're in one of these high states and you will look like the Christ. I don't care what you look like now, you'll look like the Christ.

You know what can happen just before your ascension? The whole tube of light can compress in a sense and the Presence can come down and be really close to you, right above your head. And when man ascends up into the Presence, he becomes one with it. Where's your gray hair? Where're your wrinkles? Where's fading eyesight? Where's bad hearing? Where's imperfection? Can any of this live in the heart of God? He doesn't know that it exists. So if you ascend into that, you ascend into eternal life.

THE THREEFOLD FLAME

Now during this Easter season, the whole Christian Church is stressing the crown of thorns. The *via dolorosa,* the sorrowful way, the way to Golgotha, that is what people are stressing today in the Church—that Christ died as a sacrifice for our sins.

But the Bible clearly states that "every man shall

bear his own burden."[16] And I have long said that if we were looking for a sacrifice for sins, because Adam's sin was passed on to all, the moment that Jesus said, "It is finished!" it *would* have been finished. Death would have ended for every human being and we would all have eternal life right now. It would have been done immediately.

Christ showed the example. But you don't have to get out here today and get yourself physically crucified in order to be saved. The body of man *is* a cross on which the rose of the soul is crucified. But that soul is going to rise from the cross of the body, and it will transmute the cross into the crown —not of thorns but of life.

The way that it is done is through the balancing of what we call the threefold flame of life, which is down here in the lower figure on the Chart. You will notice there is a pink plume signifying divine love, a yellow plume signifying illumination, or holy wisdom, and a blue plume signifying faith and power.

And I want to explain to all of you people in this audience that most of you do not have a balanced threefold flame. Some of you in this audience, and we can see it, have a lot of power and a lot of faith and your blue plume is big, it maybe goes clear to the ceiling. But some of you have very little love.

Some of you have a lot of love. You're so loving, you could just love the whole world. You have a great big pink plume, but a very tiny plume of illumination. You don't have a lot of real understanding yet.

Some of you have a great big plume of gold. You have all kinds of understanding, but you don't have much faith, and therefore you don't put it to work. Or you don't have much love for people, just for yourself.

What the Christ wants us to do is to balance the

threefold flame. If we're a person with great faith and great power, we're a first-ray person. He wants us to learn to love one another. He wants us to obtain wisdom. "With all thy getting get understanding."[17]

If we have a lot of worldly wisdom but very little love for the world, very little faith in the purposes of life, he wants us to gain these other two legs of being.

Our duty on earth is to balance our threefold flame and then expand the three plumes all at once —not just one aspect of being, but all of them. Because only by balancing all of them can we actually attain our fullness of Christ perfection.

THE VIOLET FIRE

We've talked about the tube of light. We've talked about the Christ Self, about the Paraclete, about the God Presence, about the causal body. Now, let's talk about the violet fire.

I will quote Jesus. He said, "I will not drink of this fruit of the vine again until I drink it new in my Father's kingdom."[18] The purple of the grape, the new wine, is the highest form of light of the rainbow. Christ represents light. And what is the highest part of light in the physical spectrum? It is the violet.

What do we see around the head of the Christ in most pictures? An aura, or a halo, or a nimbus. Most of the time it's painted white. In very high souls, people who are advanced, with huge causal bodies, it's a pale violet.

I want to explain to all of you that the violet transmuting flame is the drawing of God's energy down into your forcefield and around you. It should be about six feet in diameter and about nine feet high. There's a reason for making it bigger than your body. In cases of cancer surgery, they always take out plenty of tissue around the surgery—I'm just using that as a little illustration here. You want the violet flame to go out farther than your body, because you don't just live in your body.

Your aura actually can affect people clear across the room. And that's why you want to have that violet flame big enough that it will catch all of the fringe areas of your radiation pattern. If you don't, you may find that you are going to reinfect yourself.

Figure of Christ, by Heinrich Hofmann

You sterilize yourself with light, and then you reinfect yourself afterwards.

You want to get all this negative magnetism out of your being. How do you do it? By visualizing the violet transmuting flame as a circle around you, six feet in diameter and nine feet high. You invoke it. You have to say it. I'm going to give you an example of how you can actually put this tube of light around yourself and how you can actually create the violet flame.

I want to stress the importance of visualization. You cannot create what you cannot visualize—just as an artist cannot paint a picture that he cannot see. Therefore, you must perfect yourself in visualization, and that's one reason we have the aid of the Chart. We try to set the physical color of the Chart as close as possible to the type of vibratory action that is the true violet flame.

Then you should have an actual sense of the motion of the flame, just like physical flames, licking right up around you. This fire is not going to hurt you at all. It will do you a lot of good. So here's the way you do it.

> O my constant, loving I AM Presence, thou light of God above me whose radiance forms a circle of fire before me to light my way:
>
> I AM faithfully calling to thee to place a great pillar of light from my own mighty I AM God Presence all around me right now today! Keep it intact through every passing moment, manifesting as a shimmering shower of God's beautiful light through which nothing human can ever pass. Into this beautiful electric circle of divinely charged energy direct a swift upsurge of the violet fire of freedom's forgiving, transmuting flame!

When you say that, you are commanding light to obey you. And God is perfectly in agreement when you're doing it.

Why are you doing it? Why are you commanding light to obey you? So that the light will consume the dross.

What does the refiner do with gold? Why does he put a fire under gold and cook it and heat it up? So he can skim off the dross. And that's the purpose of the violet transmuting flame.

By age regression through hypnosis, people are finding out all kinds of things that are buried in the subconscious or in the past. You don't have to regress in age and go through the dangers of hypnotism. All you have to do is use the violet transmuting flame. And you don't have to stir up all this negative energy and bring it forth into your world today. That's Pandora's box. That's why so many people in various groups today are having so much trouble. They don't realize when they release into their worlds a putrid poison that they cannot handle.

The violet transmuting flame is safe. It's just as safe as taking communion, the Lord's Supper. It isn't going to hurt you at all, and it will do you a world of good. So when you say, "Blaze this fire up around me" and you visualize it, you can do this for five or ten minutes. You can sit there and visualize the flame.

That cuts deep. When you first start doing it, if you could see clairvoyantly, you would see hunks of black tarry substance popping right out of your being. They would come up into the flame, and you'd see them shaking in there and then you'd see them melt and then disappear as a puff of smoke.

Most people can't see this, but some of our students can. And it's a wonderful thing to see, because all through our physical bodies as a cause of disease is the accumulation of black, tarry substance that is actually negative energy that we've put in there through many embodiments.

Some of it we've put there in one embodiment. For example, if you love French-fried potatoes and you just keep on eating these things, after a while you get so much cholesterol in your body that it's like a tarry substance that's clogging your bloodstream. It makes the calcium deposits on the arterial walls. It shrinks them and narrows them down until it raises your blood pressure. Well, you can even help deal with that using the violet flame. You can benefit your whole body.

I've seen people who used the violet flame for twenty or thirty years, who were ninety years old and whose minds were as alert as somebody would be at thirty-five or forty. And I think there is a tremendous benefit to your flesh form as well as your mind and your being by using the violet flame.

FREEDOM FROM KARMA

Now what happens when you start using the violet flame over a period of time? What can you expect is going to happen to you? Purification. Karma, or negative things that you've done from past lives, is cumulative and it piles up. This violet flame is the power of transmutation or forgiveness that forgives you for past mistakes.

In the strict Christian idea of it all, you say, "Well, I'll be forgiven my sins. I'll ask God to forgive me, and he'll forgive me." Of course he does. But the Law requires that every one of us balance every bit of karma that we ever had. I can teach you that in the lesser mysteries sometime. I won't go into it now, but I want to touch on it, because it's a very important point. I hope that you can see this point as I explain it to you.

If I go out into this audience and step on someone's toe and I break it, God forbid, and I say, "I'm terribly sorry, will you forgive me?" They may say, "Of course I'll forgive you." But that doesn't stop their pain.

The Law requires that even though I'm forgiven

and it may not descend on me right then and there that I have to have my toe broken ("An eye for an eye, a tooth for a tooth"[19]), I have to balance that debt to life somehow. So there is a responsibility that we might as well share.

One of the great dangers of Christian dogma that the enemy put into the Church was this idea that your sins can be forgiven. So people went to their priests and had their sins forgiven on Sunday, and then the next Saturday night they went out and howled and did the same thing over again. They thought they were getting away with it, when in actuality they were just piling up layers and layers and layers of karma to be balanced.

That's a very important point, because we don't get away with anything. And what's more, every good thing we do we get credit for. So the universe is not such an unjust place after all, is it? All we have to do, then, is start qualifying light properly and we'll be free.

We obtain our freedom, however, in many ways. The violet transmuting flame not only dissolves the tarry substance in your physical form, it actually works through your brain and it works through the mind. And it will free the mind from a lot of the negative imperfections of the mind, wrong thoughts. It also wipes the etheric body clean. It burns up all the negative memory patterns.

A lot of people today have wrong thoughts. They think thoughts that are filthy, even though they don't want to. They can't help themselves. These thoughts will pop into their minds. And you know how the master talked about it? He said, "Well, dear people, you maybe can't help it if a bird lands on your head, but you don't have to let him build a nest in your hair."

That's the idea. But we would all like to be masters of our mind so we would never think a filthy thought—never, never, never! The violet transmuting flame will cook out the cause and core from the etheric body. That's why this flame is so enormously important.

People go to church and they go to the altar and they follow the prescribed program of religious instruction that is supposed to make them a saint, but they never seem to overcome a lot of the faults and imperfections they have. This is because these things are in their body.

Saint Paul stated it very clearly: "For the good that I would I do not: and the evil which I would not, that I do. . . . But I see another law working in my members."[20] And this law working in our members, which is residual substance from embodiment after embodiment of imperfection, can be absolutely cooked out of us with these decrees.

I have seen people in six months of decree work change their whole countenance. We had a man in our group here that came from skid row. I'm not going to tell you what kind of a man he was. He certainly wasn't a good man. And he went into decrees and he decreed for approximately two months and his whole countenance changed. He was the most seedy-looking character you ever saw, and he actually improved tremendously in two months—until he went into the psychic. He quit coming to decree services and he quit using the violet flame and he went downhill, right back into the same boat he was in before.

So you see, the violet transmuting flame is

something that you have to keep on keeping on with. And that is not really a bad thing at all. I know myself that if someone had asked me to a dinner and I really wanted to enjoy myself at that dinner, if I were to use the violet flame before I went to eat, that I would feel a great deal better. And I mean just that. I would feel physically stronger. My taste buds would be working better. Everything in my world would be better because I used the violet flame.

The violet flame even helps you physically. And if you have a talk you're going to give to a group, you're called upon as a business or professional man, if you use the violet flame before you get up to give that talk, you can clear a lot of musty concepts out of your world and you can have a lot more power of extemporaneous speaking because you don't have all that residual substance.

Keep your tube of light around yourself to insulate yourself from the audience, which is a very important thing because an audience can ruin you or they can make you. The violet transmuting flame and the tube of light are two of the most important things.

YOU ARE NEVER ALONE

So in way of review, here is your tube of light. Here is your human figure. Here is the threefold flame. Here is the silver cord connecting you with your God Presence. Here are the mighty light rays that connect your God Presence with every other God Presence in the universe.

And this is going to be an interesting thing. You are never alone. You are *never* alone! Because every causal body is connected with every other causal body through mighty light rays that reach out in the universe and join hands.

It's like the whole cosmos stretched out here with stars and suns and planets without number. And they're all linked together as one great network of light. Isn't that a beautiful thing? So you are never alone. You're always connected above. Of course, down here people get connected in snake dances too—we don't want that.

You have in this Chart the whole story of yourself and your relationship to God. You have the means to get out of the human octave through the violet transmuting flame.

This great God Presence is the real you and it is beautiful. Saint Germain has said that this Chart is only a symbol. But he says that it's a mighty symbol because it helps you to realize yourself and your potential.

- 4 -

THE THREEFOLD FLAME

Saint Germain

Your heart is one of the choicest gifts of God. Within it there is a central chamber surrounded by a forcefield of such light and protection that we call it a "cosmic interval."

It is a chamber separated from Matter, and no probing could ever discover it. It occupies, simultaneously, not only the third and fourth dimensions but also other dimensions unknown to man. It is thus the connecting point of the mighty crystal cord of light that descends from your God Presence to sustain the beating of your physical heart, giving you life, purpose, and cosmic integration.

I urge you to treasure this point of contact that you have with life by paying conscious recognition to it. You do not need to understand by sophisticated language or scientific postulation the how, why, and wherefore of this activity. Be content to know that God is there and that there is within you a point of contact with the Divine, a spark of fire from the Creator's own heart that is called the threefold flame of life. There it burns as the triune essence of love, wisdom, and power.

Each acknowledgment paid daily to the flame within your heart will amplify the power and illumination of love within your being. Each such attention will produce a new sense of dimension for you, if not outwardly apparent then subconsciously manifest within the folds of your inner thoughts.

Neglect not, then, your heart as the altar of God. Neglect it not as the sun of your manifest being. Draw from God the power of love and amplify it within your heart. Then send it out into the world at large as the bulwark of that which shall overcome the darkness of the planet, saying:

I AM the light of the heart
Shining in the darkness of being
And changing all into the golden treasury
Of the mind of Christ.

I AM projecting my love
Out into the world
To erase all errors
And to break down all barriers.

I AM the power of infinite love,
Amplifying itself
Until it is victorious,
World without end!

With this gift of infinite freedom, I give you my never-ending promise to assist you to find your immortal freedom as you determine never to give up and never to turn back.

Remember that as long as you face the light, the shadows are always behind. And the light is there, too, to transmute them all.

- 5 -

HEALING THOUGHTFORMS FOR YOUR HEART

Elizabeth Clare Prophet

One of the greatest gifts of identity, which the conscious mind little dreams of, is the latent ability to realize the image of the eye. This science of the immaculate concept is practiced by every angel in heaven.

It is that law which is written in the inward parts of man,[1] known by his very heart of hearts, yet dim in the memory of his outer mind. It is based on the visualization of a perfect idea, which then becomes a magnet that attracts the creative energies of the Holy Spirit to his being to fulfill the pattern held in mind.

Having seen what he is in Spirit and what is the potential of his soul, man must retain that image of reality in his thoughts and feelings, for the image is a natural repellent to all that opposes his reality in manifestation. This he does through the real eye of his soul—his inner eye that knows as it sees and sees as it knows.

The eye magic of the soul is the *I-mage* or image of reality which man plants in his consciousness and waters with the pure energies that flow freely from the Macrocosm. The increase of the abundant life that follows is the LORD's, or the Law's. For those who follow the scientific principle of the real-eye magic find that they are rewarded by the same. As Saint Paul said, "I have planted, Apollos watered; but God gave the increase."[2]

And so God is expressed impersonally in the outworking of his immutable laws, all of which are corollary to the one Great Law of being in cosmos. The science of the immaculate concept, then, is the knowledge of how to use pure ideas to transform the world of the microcosm into a macrocosmic wonder—*as Above in God, so below in man.*

SEEDS OF LIGHT

Beauty and truth have a geometry all their own, a symmetry that allows the energies of God to flow freely through their ideations and then to coalesce in form. Pure ideas and noble forms are the archetypal patterns of the Real Image. They are seeds of light which, when planted in the subconscious and conscious domains of the fertile mind, bring forth after their kind. Without these kernels of light, rooted and nourished in the very substance of his soul, man cannot hope to express perfection in his world.

Each one is a lodestone of God-desire to become without, all that which is within. Each one is a magnet that attracts from God above to man below the creative essence of the universe. And if these monads be abundantly scattered throughout his consciousness—each one a nucleus of Reality, each one a forcefield of fervent faith, hope, and charity —then man can indeed look to *outpicture* (manifest) in the microcosm that which he has thought to be "the impossible dream, the unreachable star."

Each time the soul beholds the sun, the clouds, the wind in the trees, a rose, a perfect leaf, a pebble, or a wave, and then tucks the design in the folds of memory, he is adding to his treasure of those perfect ideas which are the building blocks of his reality.

Michelangelo's *David*

Each time the fingers of his mind trace the lines of a Michelangelo, the strokes of a Raphael, the movements of a symphony, the cadences of a ballet, the formations of the birds that cross the sky, the soul takes in the patterns of the mind of God on which hang the entire schemata of his microcosmic universe.

Beholding the universe and even our own

planetary home, we observe how nature upholds the law of perfection and shrugs off imperfection. Truly, the very stones that cry out in praise of the Christ do uphold more earnestly than man his mandate: "Be ye therefore perfect, even as your Father which is in heaven is perfect."[3]

How beautifully the LORD has placed all around us in the natural kingdom these links to eternity and to the invisible world of realities that we perceive only in the substance of things hoped for—these precious evidences of things not seen![4]

THE CHRIST FLAME

The Christ flame within the heart embodies the same qualities of love, wisdom, and power that manifest in the heart of the Almighty, in the heart of your I AM Presence, and in the heart of your Christ Self.

Right within your own body temple are three fiery plumes of the Holy Spirit—pink, yellow, and blue pulsations of living flame. Thus the heavenly Trinity gains expression in the world of material form. And the energies of Father (blue), Son (yellow), and Holy Spirit (pink) are resplendent in the heart of man.

Also corresponding with the trinity of body, mind, and soul, the threefold flame supplies man's needs for power to run the body (the faith and goodwill of the divine intent); wisdom to nourish the mind (illumination and the right use of the knowledge of the Law); and love to fulfill the destiny of the soul in conscious outer manifestation (a just and merciful compassion that is always rewarded by individual creative fulfillment).

The flame within the heart is your personal focus of the sacred fire. It is your opportunity to become the Christ. It is the potential of your divinity waiting to burst into being within your humanity.

During the first three golden ages, before man's departure from innocence, the crystal cord was nine feet in diameter and the threefold flame enveloped his form. Man's source of energy was literally unlimited and his Christ consciousness was all-enfolding.

After the Fall, man's opportunity to exercise his free will was curtailed. By cosmic edict the threefold flame was reduced to one-sixteenth of an inch in height.

Imbalance—where giantism occurs in one aspect of the threefold flame, causing it to be out of proportion to the others—prevents the achievement of the goal of individual Christ-mastery.

As the flame of illumination expands from within your consciousness, it gradually enfolds your being until God, as holy wisdom, is enthroned upon the altar of your heart. But with each increase of wisdom, the power and love plumes must also rise by the fiat of your devotion; else the wisdom will not be retained.

Likewise, with each getting of power there must come the attainment of wisdom and love in perfect balance. So, too, love is actualized only through an equivalent manifestation of power and wisdom.

Recognizing that balance is the golden key to Christhood, you must understand that you cannot know for yourself or bring into manifestation that which you have not first realized within the threefold flame as the result of your outer and inner experience in God.

Start by visualizing the threefold flame within your heart, one-sixteenth of an inch in height, sealed within the secret chamber of your heart. Then watch it expand and expand and expand as you meditate on love.

A MANTRA FOR THE RESURRECTION FLAME

**I AM the resurrection and the life
of every cell and atom of my heart
now made manifest!**

Whenever you pronounce the name of God "I AM"—which was given to Moses for our blessing[5]—as the affirmation of God's own being where you are, you are really saying, "God in me is . . . "

So in this mantra you are actually acknowledging: "God in me is the resurrection and the life of every cell and atom of my heart now made manifest!"

Because "I AM" is the sacred name as well as the verb "to be," we understand our God to be a living, ongoing, dynamic reality—a most personal Presence who reveals himself to us in action in our individual lives and in his miraculous yet entirely scientific flow of light, light, light!

God wants us to affirm our being as his, and his as our very own. It is our fiery destiny to be one—that is, to share in his universal oneness. This we accomplish day by day by confirming his Word—"I AM"—in our mantras.

The science of the spoken Word is the means to our soul's union with Spirit. If you don't believe it, prove it for yourself! Give your mantra for the resurrection and the life of your heart many times a day. Enjoy it! For God's energy enjoys the mighty work of making you whole. And he wants you to enjoy a fruitful life as you serve to set all life free.

> And it shall come to pass, that before they call, I will answer; and while they are yet speaking, I will hear.
> —ISAIAH

The resurrection flame, the acceleration of the threefold flame that is released in this effective fiat, was used by Jesus the Christ in his victory over death and hell. He came to show you the way so that you could do the same through Christ who lives in you as your own Real Self. What are you waiting for? Say it out loud with all your heart:

I AM the resurrection and the life
of every cell and atom of my heart
now made manifest!

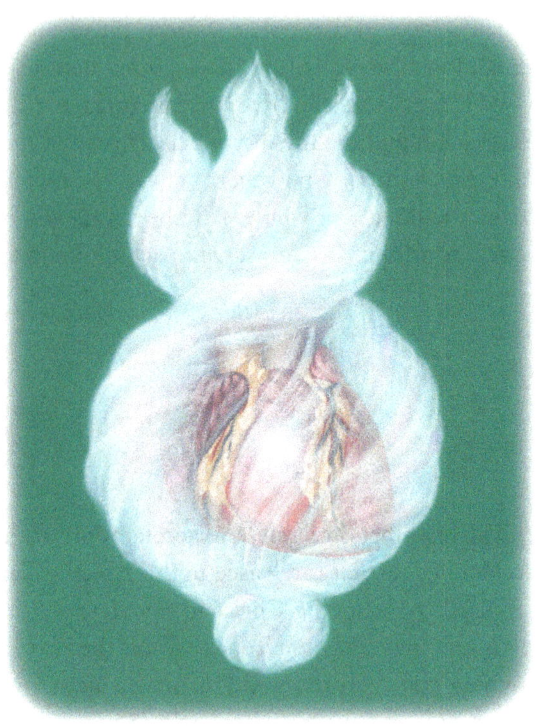

Visualize the swirling mother-of-pearl stream of
resurrection's flame bathing and invigorating your heart.
Feel its regenerative power restoring the rhythm
and beauty of flow in your lifestream.

The resurrection flame can be felt as a radiant, mother-of-pearl softness, bathing the body in a gentle, suffusing glow. As it accelerates with the ritual of your daily application, the rainbow rays merge into the white light.

Our beloved Jesus gave us the "I AM" affirmation—"I AM the resurrection and the life . . . "[6]—to use for any condition or situation that has gone awry from the original intent of our Father. So you can say:

I AM the resurrection and the life
of my perfect health now made manifest!

By all means, you should be very specific in naming the part or parts of the body. Always affirm the perfection desired in place of the imperfect manifestation:

I AM the resurrection and the life of the
inner blueprint of ___(Insert names of body parts that have been affected)___
now made manifest!

Now that you have set the matrix of your "I AM" affirmation, give and learn by heart another beautiful affirmation of the Lord's eternal spirit of the resurrection everywhere present where you are —but especially in your members that need healing and wholeness:

> I AM the flame of resurrection
> Blazing God's pure light through me
> Now I AM raising every atom,
> From every shadow I AM free!
>
> I AM the light of God's full presence,
> I AM living ever free.
> Now the flame of life eternal
> Rises up to victory!

The flame of the resurrection (a stepped-up version of your threefold flame) is invoked for the resurgence of life whenever the flow of life is interfered with or abruptly cut off, whether at the molecular level or within the organic bodies of entire communities and nations or in the environment of elemental life. Its colorful crystals are the cupbearers of renewal, rebirth, rejuvenation, and restoration.

Passing through atoms, cells, and electrons, the flame transmits the spin of your soul's joie de vivre, restoring the natural rhythm of your unique life cycles. Beginning with your heartbeat, then activating the pulsation of billions of atomic nuclei and sun-centers of your cells, it regulates the figure-eight flow of spiritual energies in and out of your matter universe.

The resurrection flame is the fount of bubbling joy that brings the smile of spiritual satisfaction to your face because you experience that inner awareness of your never-ending reason for being.

Visualize yourself standing in a pillar of swirling, opalescent rainbow spirals. Through the "I AM" name and the resurrection flame, you know who you are because you *know* who God is.

A THOUGHTFORM FOR PURIFICATION

The inner eye of your soul can penetrate atomic particles and adjust cellular structure.

Visualize a stream of yellow light passing through and washing every cell of your heart. All toxic accumulations are removed as each cell receives the currents of healing light from the heart of Alpha and Omega in the Great Central Sun.

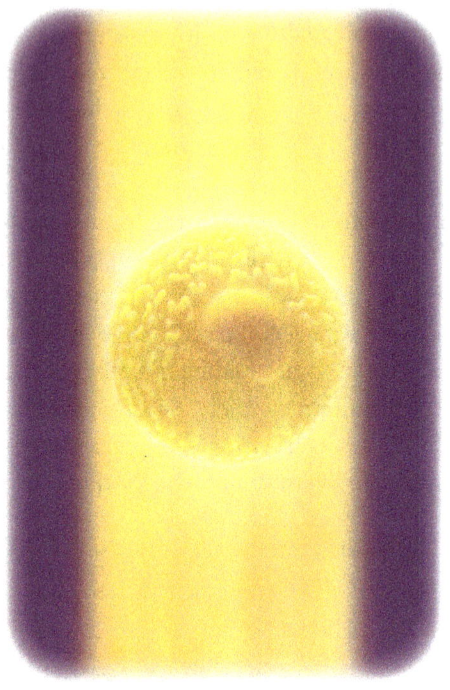

A gentle bath of liquid light purifies a white blood cell within the heart.

You can also apply your visualization to the water molecule.

Water is the carrier for all the elements of the bloodstream and comprises over two-thirds of your body weight. The water molecule is shown in its tetrahedral configuration formed by the chemical bonding of two hydrogen atoms and a central oxygen atom. (There is a slight distortion in the tetrahedral shape of the molecule because of the presence of hydrogen nuclei in only two of the four electron clouds of the oxygen atom.)

Now visualize the hydrogen atom bathed in purifying light. The single proton of the nucleus is surrounded by a spherical energy shell, or "probability cloud," where the electron is found.

THE STRENGTHENING OF THE AURA

One of the first exercises for the strengthening of the aura involves a threefold action. The student begins by visualizing the threefold flame expanding from within his heart; he then seals himself and his consciousness in a globe of white fire; and when he is set, he proceeds to recite the following words with utter humility and devotion:

I AM light, glowing light,
Radiating light, intensified light.
God consumes my darkness,
Transmuting it into light.

This day I AM a focus of the Central Sun.
Flowing through me is a crystal river,
A living fountain of light
That can never be qualified
By human thought and feeling.
I AM an outpost of the Divine.
Such darkness as has used me is swallowed up
By the mighty river of light which I AM.

I AM, I AM, I AM light;
I live, I live, I live in light.
I AM light's fullest dimension;
I AM light's purest intention.
I AM light, light, light
Flooding the world everywhere I move,
Blessing, strengthening, and conveying
The purpose of the kingdom of heaven.

As you visualize the white-fire radiance around yourself, do not be concerned with the errors in your thought that through the years may have intruded themselves upon your consciousness. Do not allow yourself to concentrate upon any negative quality or condition. Do not let your attention rest upon your supposed imperfections.

Instead, see what the light can do for you. See how even your physical form can change, how a strengthening of the bonds of your health can occur in body, mind, and spirit.

Try this exercise, simple though it may seem, and know that many ascended beings will be performing it with you.

A MANTRA FOR CHRIST WHOLENESS

Now you are ready to give your mantra for Christ wholeness. Use it to "make a joyful noise unto the LORD," as the Psalmist himself burst forth in praise.[7]

Let the praise of *your* soul come before his presence with the singing of this mantra. Serve him with the gladness of his perfection manifest in you now!

> Know ye that the LORD he is God: it is he that hath made us, and not we ourselves.
> —PSALMS

God made you perfect. Restore yourself to that perfection God-willed. Stand fast and behold the salvation of your God. Then "clap your hands" and "shout unto God with the voice of triumph!"

Now give this dynamic decree to your beloved I AM Presence, to your blessed Christ Self, and to the healing masters and angels of the sacred fire with all your heart:

1. I AM God's perfection manifest
In body, mind, and soul—
I AM God's direction flowing
To heal and keep me whole!

Refrain:

O atoms, cells, electrons
  Within this form of mine,
Let heaven's own perfection
  Make me now divine!

The spirals of Christ wholeness
  Enfold me by his might—
I AM the Master Presence
  Commanding, "Be all light!"

2. I AM God's perfect image:
  My form is charged by love;
Let shadows now diminish,
  Be blessed by Comfort's Dove!

3. O blessed Jesus, Master dear,
  Send thy ray of healing here;
Fill me with thy life above,
  Raise me in thine arms of love!

4. I AM Christ's healing Presence,
  All shining like a mercy sun—
I AM that pure perfection,
  My perfect healing won!

5. I charge and charge and charge myself
  With radiant I AM light—
I feel the flow of purity
  That now makes all things right!

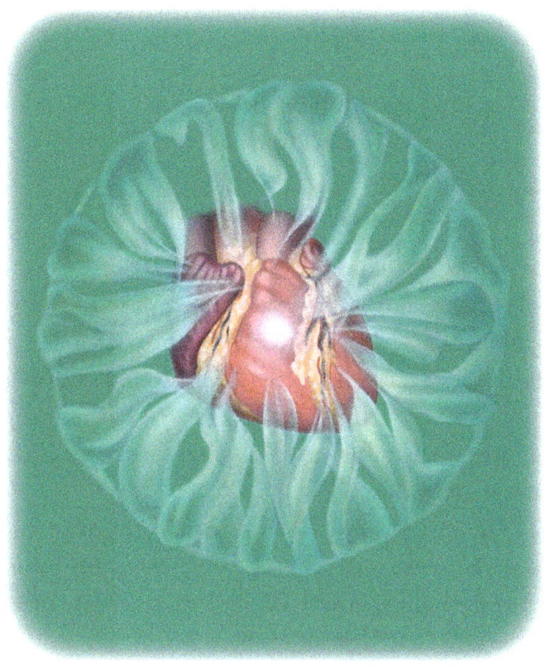

As you give the mantra for Christ wholeness,
visualize the healing flame of nature's life-giving forces
penetrating in, through, and around your heart.
Feel the emerald ray restoring the scientific matrix
of body, mind, and soul.

A VIOLET-FIRE MANTRA FOR THE HEART

Violet fire, thou love divine,
Blaze within this heart of mine!
Thou art mercy forever true,
Keep me always in tune with you.

When we make a heart contact with the Person and Presence of the Holy Spirit, by purest love we may tap the source of the sacred fire of God. For the Spirit of the LORD is the agent of God's healing, while the sacred fire is the agency. Through his Holy Spirit, God releases his great love to us as the energy of *change*.

The quickest way to flush out the cause and core of disease is to apply the unguent of the transforming light of the Holy Spirit. And the violet flame is the instrument of the fiery baptism of that very personal and very present Spirit.

It is the flow of God's unfailing mercy and forgiveness. It is the "refiner's fire" for the purging of the sons of God prophesied by Malachi.[8]

When you invoke the violet flame with joy and

full faith in God's promise—"I will forgive their iniquity, and I will remember their sin no more"[9]—you can feel the pulsating alchemical action of the LORD's "universal solvent" dissolving the cause and the effect, the record and the cell memory of all physical imperfections and impurities outcropping from the conscious and subconscious planes of your being.

Your call, confidently and lovingly given *aloud,* is the exercise of the science of the *spoken* Word. *The call,* by your free will, sets in motion the *flow* of the violet fire that transmutes the underlying emotional and mental conditions that are causative in all disease.

But you must also willingly submit to the flame such manifestations as anger and aggravation, hatred and even mild dislike toward any part of life or person—even subtle resentment held in your heart against yourself or members of your family.

The healing of all hardness of heart—which *must go* before physical healing and wholeness can take place—requires the unconditional surrender of your soul to your beloved Christ Self. Stubborn will and human pride *must go* into the flame!

For the expansion of your heart's physical and spiritual capacity, give your violet-fire heart mantra many times over with your strongest and most concentrated visualization—for and by the love of Jesus Christ. Practice makes perfect.

Remember, all layers of your consciousness are affected by the pure flow of light directly from the heart of your Christ Self to and through your physical heart. Persistence is needed to penetrate age-old habits of human discord resulting in "men's hearts failing them for fear."[10]

Healing is a letting-go process. Do it every day as you bid the Lord welcome into your heart. Express the sunshine of self-givingness to someone who needs your love *every day.*

As you flush out the old toxins of ingratitude toward life and rebellion against the wonderful law of universal harmony, let your heart burst forth in these cadences of joyous communion:

O mighty Presence of God, I AM,
in and behind the Sun:
I welcome thy Light,
which floods all the earth,
into my life, into my mind,
into my spirit, into my soul!
Radiate and blaze forth thy Light!
Break the bonds of darkness
and superstition!
Charge me with the great clearness
of thy white fire radiance!
I AM thy child, and each day I shall become
more of thy manifestation!

Now *be still and know* that the "I AM" Presence who is God within you (the Immanuel—*God with us*) is victorious over every outer condition. Accept it done in the full power of the Godhead and reaffirm it each time the slightest fear or doubt assails your soul:

> "I AM" the violet-flame miracle healing of my heart every hour of every day now made manifest! And I praise the Lord of life for my perfect healing now made manifest!

Visualize the violet flame of freedom and forgiveness transmuting all impurities in your heart—physical, mental, emotional, and etheric.

THE HEALING THOUGHTFORM

The healing thoughtform is another gift of God's love, scientifically formulated to remagnetize and restore the elements of your four lower bodies to nature's design.

The healing thoughtform is composed of concentric spheres of God's healing light—a sphere of white surrounded by a sphere of blue suspended within a globe of green.

Whenever you pray for healing, know that *the call compels the answer.* Then call upon the LORD and *know* that he will answer:

> In the name of Jesus Christ and his presence with me in the Person of my own Christ Self, I call to the heart of my own beloved I AM Presence and the angels of healing for the beautiful healing thoughtform to seal me in the perfect light of God's own consciousness of my wholeness—*now made manifest!*

Then visualize spheres of sacred fire descending as the pulsating presence of the Holy Spirit. Visualize the white-fire core centered in the scintillating,

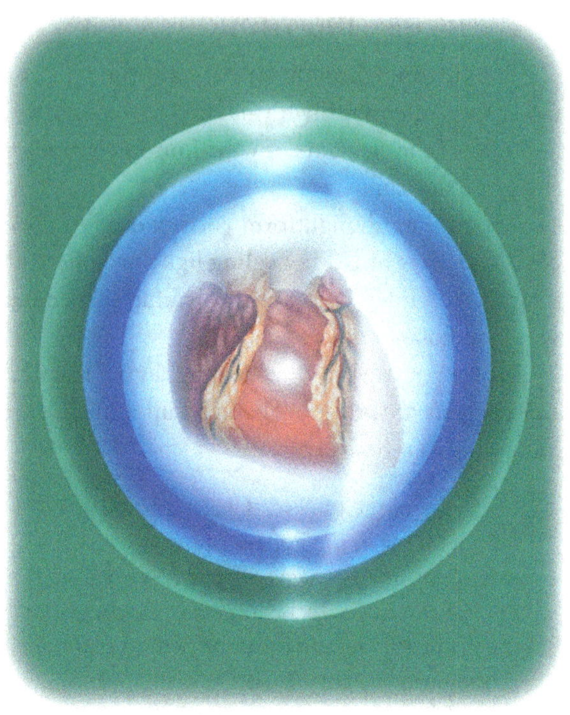

Visualize the white, blue, and green spheres of God's sacred fire surrounding and penetrating every atom, cell, and electron of your physical heart, restoring the inner blueprint and divine wholeness of your life.

sapphire-blue flame wrapped in the leaping, emerald-green fires.

By your unspeakable love for the Holy Spirit, magnetize this healing thoughtform from the mind of God—first to your heart and then to any distressed, disturbed, or diseased area of the body. You can even see your entire form enfolded in God's healing presence—for when your eye is single (your visualization concentrated and charged with love), your whole body shall be full of light. It is the LORD's promise, and he will not fail you.

> The light of the body is the eye: if therefore thine eye be single, thy whole body shall be full of light.
> —JESUS

The healing process takes place through the restoration of Christ's wholeness—first in your soul (both spiritually and emotionally), then in your mind (mentally and visually), and finally in your body, which will always reflect the state of your higher vehicles.

The white-fire core, always interacting with the violet flame, is the energy of Alpha and Omega that transmutes the conditions (physical, mental, and emotional) that cause the disorder—that is, the *dis-ordering* of the altogether natural flow of harmony in your life.

The blue sphere—again in combination with the violet fire—is the action of the will of God which summons by divine decree the atoms, molecules, and cells into conformity with the inner blueprint of the Son of God in whose image you were and are "fearfully and wonderfully made."

With this realization you ought to shout for joy with the Psalmist, who said: "I will praise thee, for *I AM* fearfully and wonderfully made!"[11]

The green sphere—blending with the scrubbing, scouring action of the violet flame—is the miracle of God's immortal life that restores the flow of Spirit through Matter and makes it whole. *See* in your mind's eye the healing thoughtform alternating with the surging/resurging violet flame, burning through all substance blocking the flow of the life force.

As the whirling (clockwise) thoughtform magnetizes the flow of your lifestream into the matrix of nature's original design, the debris of centuries of misqualified thought and feeling substance is thrown off, by centrifugal force, into the violet flame, where it is stripped of all discord and transmuted by the alchemy of the Holy Spirit back to the crystal clarity of the River of Life.

- 6 -

THE POWER OF THOUGHT

The Editors

In this book we have explored some of the spiritual science of thoughtforms. Mark Prophet has shown how to use thoughtforms to expand awareness beyond the normal bounds of the human mind, giving a glimpse of the cosmic consciousness that is our birthright.

Elizabeth Clare Prophet has outlined the use of thoughtforms for physical healing. These techniques can similarly be used for healing the mind, the emotions and the etheric body—and by expanding the sphere of our awareness, healing the world around us.

Clearly, what is in this volume is just the beginning of the power of thought to change our lives.

This is not a new idea, of course. Ella Wheeler Wilcox, beloved poet and student of metaphysics early in the twentieth century, wrote a short poem on the power of thought:

Thoughts Are Things

You can never tell what your thoughts will do
In bringing you hate or love,
For thoughts are things, and their airy wings
Are swift as a carrier dove.

They follow the law of the universe—
Each thing must create its kind—
And they speed o'er the track to bring you back
Whatever went out from your mind.

The reality of thought may be less obvious than the reality of the seemingly concrete world around us. Yet creations on the mental plane are no less real. Thoughts really *are* things on the plane of their existence. But that is not the limit to their reality.

According to the law of return, the law of karma, the thoughts we send out into the world return to us. If we send out love and blessings to the world, this energy will return to us. If we send out anger or hatred, this energy will also eventually return to us in some way. Furthermore, as emotional and physical energy coalesces around the matrix of mental substance, the energy returning may also manifest physically.

One example is the profound effect of thought on the physical body. Researchers in the emerging field of mind-body medicine are beginning to understand how many diseases have their origins in the mind, and conversely, the profound power of the mind to heal the body.[1]

This is just the beginning of the power of thought. Saint Germain has taught extensively on the use of thoughtforms for physical creation. In his "Studies in Alchemy," he outlines nine steps in an alchemical formula for precipitation.[2] These begin with a detailed mental thoughtform that is created and held in consciousness until the object visualized becomes a physical reality—either by direct precipitation from the Universal or by indirect means.

The time taken for the return of the energy we

send out depends on many factors. Sometimes we can experience good or bad karma almost instantaneously. We get angry, and we stub our toe. Sometimes the things we experience in life are the result of thoughtforms we sent out decades ago or in a previous lifetime. There are long and short cycles of karma, and even though our karma may be set aside for a time by the law of mercy and forgiveness, reaping what we sow is always the law of nature and of nature's God.

If we have created unwisely, we will find burdens of various sorts coming upon us—mental, emotional, or physical. By using the science of thoughtforms, we can transmute the manifestations we created foolishly or ignorantly in the past. And we can create new thoughtforms that will manifest in a far brighter future.

We invite you to begin your own experiments with this science. Like learning any new skill—playing a musical instrument or taking up a new sport—regular practice will lead to tangible results. The universe doesn't yield all its secrets the moment we step on the Path.

But if you desire to pursue this path, the door is open. As you build a momentum on the use of creative thoughtforms, you can expect to see many changes in your life. You may well find, as many others have before you, that life becomes a sacred adventure.

NOTES

CHAPTER 1 • The Use of Thoughtforms in the Expansion of Consciousness

1. In a dictation on May 31, 1964, God Meru said: "Precious ones, if your consciousness were as small as a thimble and the tube of radiant light which pours down from above as small as a needle, if you persisted long enough, you could fill the thimble and then call for more light to enlarge it to the size of a barrel and then to a great lake, and then further expand it without limit simply because you yourselves were diligent in the service of the light."
2. Matt. 10:42.
3. Gen. 1:26.
4. Gen. 1:28.
5. II Pet. 3:5.
6. John 5:30; 14:10.
7. I Cor. 2:7.
8. See Baird Spalding, *Life and Teachings of the Masters of the Far East,* 6 vols. (Devorss & Co., 1986).
9. Ps. 51:5.
10. Ps. 82:6.

CHAPTER 2 • Plus Is Greater

1. The parable of the pounds is found in Luke 19:12–27. A similar parable, usually described as the parable of the talents, is found in Matt. 25:14–30.

2. Matt. 25:29; Luke 19:26.
3. John 5:17.
4. Eph. 4:28.

CHAPTER 3 • The Chart of Your Real Self—the Highest Thoughtform

1. Luke 4:29.
2. Matt. 24:23–24; Mark 13:21–22; Luke 17:21.
3. Rev. 1:8.
4. I Cor. 15:41–42.
5. Matt. 6:20.
6. Shakespeare, *The Merchant of Venice,* act 4, scene 1, lines 190–93.
7. Ecclesiastes 12:6–7 reads, "Or ever the silver cord be loosed, or the golden bowl be broken, or the pitcher be broken at the fountain, or the wheel broken at the cistern. Then shall the dust return to the earth as it was: and the spirit shall return unto God who gave it." These verses are referenced in a number of different Christian hymns, including "Saved by Grace," by Fanny Crosby (1891); "The Silver Cord Is Loosened," by Margaret Clarkson (1967); and "The Spirit Shall Return," by J. E. Kitchens (1959).
8. Matt. 22:10–13.
9. Shakespeare, *Hamlet,* act 3, scene 1, line 57.
10. John 1:1–3.
11. John 8:58.
12. Matt. 28:18.
13. Hab. 1:13.
14. James 4:8.
15. Matt. 17:1–8; Mark 9:2–8; Luke 9:28–36.

16. Gal. 6:5.
17. Prov. 4:7.
18. Matt. 26:29; Mark 14:25; Luke 22:18.
19. Matt. 5:38.
20. Rom. 7:19, 23.

CHAPTER 5 • Healing Thoughtforms for Your Heart

1. Jer. 31:33.
2. I Cor. 3:6.
3. Matt. 5:48.
4. Heb. 11:1.
5. Exod. 3:14.
6. John 11:25.
7. Pss. 98:4; 100:1.
8. Mal. 3:2.
9. Jer. 31:34.
10. Luke 21:26.
11. Ps. 139:14.

CHAPTER 6 • The Power of Thought

1. The Center for Integrative Medicine at UC Davis lists the following medical conditions for which mind-body approaches can be helpful: anxiety, heart arrhythmias, cancer, coronary artery disease, chronic pain, depression, gastrointestinal conditions, hypertension, insomnia, menopause symptoms, multiple sclerosis, psoriasis, rheumatoid arthritis, and other autoimmune conditions. https://health.ucdavis.edu/integrative-medicine/clinical-care/mind-body-medicine.html
2. See *Saint Germain On Alchemy*, Book One.

112 pp • ISBN 978-0-922729-42-5

The Creative Power of Sound

Affirmations to Create, Heal and Transform

Recent scientific advances point to what mystics have known for thousands of years: sound holds the key to the creation of the universe—and it can create spiritual and material change in our lives. Prayer is the sound and language of the soul. When spoken out loud, it can unlock the dynamic energy of the spirit. In *The Creative Power of Sound,* you will learn seven principles for applying prayers, mantras and affirmations to your everyday life. You will discover an effective way to harness spiritual energy to create positive change for yourself and the world around you.

112 pp • ISBN 978-0-922729-37-1

Violet Flame

To Heal Body, Mind and Soul

"The violet flame is a light that serves all spiritual heritages, that gives respect and dignity to all things. It gives us a way to connect with each other.... It's what really empowers you."

—Dannion Brinkley, author of *Saved by the Light*

Twentieth-century seer Edgar Cayce recognized the healing power of the violet light. Dannion Brinkley saw and experienced the violet flame in his near-death sojourns. Healers and alchemists have used this high-frequency spiritual energy to bring about energetic balance and spiritual transformation. Now you can learn how to apply the practical techniques in this book to create balance, harmony and positive change in body, mind and soul.

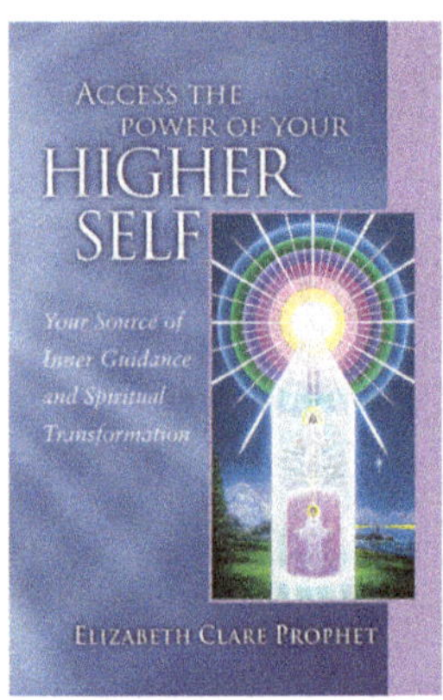

112 pp • ISBN 978-0-922729-36-4

Access the Power of Your Higher Self

Your Source of Inner Guidance and Spiritual Transformation

Access the Power of Your Higher Self presents simple techniques that can help you develop a close, working relationship with Spirit—and experience the joy, peace and empowerment that are your spiritual birthright. When you are in tune with your Higher Self, you become more loving and sensitive to your own and others' needs. You fulfill your life's purpose and express your greatest creativity. Learn ten dynamic steps to spiritual awakening that will help you realize your full potential.

Mark L. Prophet and Elizabeth Clare Prophet are world-renowned authors, spiritual teachers, and pioneers in practical spirituality. Their groundbreaking books have been published in more than thirty languages and over three million copies have been sold worldwide.

For more information about the work of Mark and Elizabeth Prophet, including their Pocket Guides to Practical Spirituality and their series on the Lost Teachings of Jesus and the Mystical Paths of the World's Religions, visit SummitUniversityPress.com.

The Summit Lighthouse®
63 Summit Way, Gardiner, Montana 59030 USA

Se habla español.

TSLinfo@TSL.org • SummitLighthouse.org
www.ElizabethClareProphet.com
1-800-245-5445 / 406-848-9500

CPSIA information can be obtained
at www.ICGtesting.com
Printed in the USA
JSHW031639190622
27064JS00003B/10